MINDFUL MONEY MANAGEMENT

Balancing Wealth And
Well-Being

JOHN DOLLAR

Copyright © 2024

by

John dollar

Table of content

INTRODUCTION

Once upon a time in the bustling town of Serenityville lived a group of friends who were determined to master the art of careful money management. The foursome consisted of Emma, a savvy businesswoman; Alex, the tech geek; Maya, an aspiring artist; and Liam, a pragmatic accountant. They realized that despite their diverse backgrounds, they have a common goal - financial freedom.

Their journey began when they came across a workshop called "Mindful Money Mastery" led by a mysterious financial guru, Professor Wisehart. Intrigued, the friends decided to embark on this journey together, each bringing their own unique skills.

The first lesson was about understanding their relationship with money. Professor Wisehart led them through introspective exercises and helped them uncover their beliefs and attitudes about finance. Emma discovered her tendency to overspend on unnecessary business investments, while Maya acknowledged her fear of overpricing her art. Alex realized that he had a habit of impulsive technology purchases, and Liam admitted that he was too conservative and avoided any risk.

Armed with self-awareness, the group moved on to the next phase of their financial quest – setting clear and achievable goals. Emma envisioned expanding her business, Alex aimed to create a tech startup, Maya dreamed of exhibiting her art in prestigious galleries, and Liam yearned to build a solid investment portfolio.

Professor Wisehart emphasized the importance of creating a budget in line with their goals. Together, the friends designed a comprehensive plan that took into account their income, expenses and savings. They learned to allocate funds for essentials, allocate a portion for personal enjoyment, and set aside savings for future ventures.

As the weeks passed, the quartet faced various challenges and tested their newfound knowledge.

Tempted by a flashy marketing campaign, Emma remembered her commitment to mindful spending and resisted the urge to invest impulsively. In a sea of technological advancement, Alex stuck to his business plan and did not deviate from the path he outlined. Faced with the opportunity to undervalue her art, Maya was adamant that her work be properly appreciated. Lured by a seemingly lucrative but risky investment, Liam weighed the potential gains against the potential losses and decided wisely to diversify.

Their devotion to mindfulness was not only reflected in their financial decisions, but also extended to their daily lives. The group practiced gratitude, appreciating what they had achieved instead of constantly seeking more. They began to enjoy simple pleasures that did not burden their wallets.

A surprise awaited them in the middle of the road. Professor Wisehart arranged for a guest speaker - a successful entrepreneur who mastered careful money management and achieved financial freedom. The speaker shared personal stories of triumphs and pitfalls and offered invaluable insights. Inspired, the friends felt a renewed sense of determination to continue their pursuit of financial well-being.

With the change of seasons, the financial situation of Emma, Alex, Maya and Liam has also changed. Emma's business expanded and generated profits that allowed her to reinvest wisely. Alex's tech startup took off and attracted investors who saw the potential in his innovative ideas. Maya's art gained recognition and she secured lucrative commissions. Liam's diversified investment portfolio flourished and provided financial stability.

With success came responsibility to return. Remembering the lessons of mindfulness, the foursome decided to use their wealth not only for personal gain, but also to make a positive impact on their community. They have initiated programs to support local businesses, mentor budding entrepreneurs, fund arts education and promote financial literacy.

Ultimately, the friends realized that careful money management is not just about accumulating possessions; it was a holistic approach to life. It included understanding one's own values, setting meaningful goals, making informed decisions, and using financial success as a tool for positive change. Looking back on their transformational journey, Emma, Alex, Maya and Liam know that the real wealth they've gained is not just in their bank accounts, but in the enriched lives they now lead.

Mindful money management is a holistic approach to managing finances that goes beyond traditional budgeting and savings practices. It involves cultivating a heightened awareness and intentional relationship with one's financial resources. This concept draws inspiration from mindfulness, a philosophy rooted in the present and fully engaging in the current moment. In the context of money, mindfulness encourages individuals to observe their spending habits, emotions, and attitudes toward wealth without judgment.

At its core, mindful money management combines the principles of mindfulness with practical financial strategies that help individuals make conscious and informed decisions about their money. It emphasizes the importance of understanding your financial goals, values and priorities and aligning them with your spending and saving patterns. By developing a deep awareness of the financial choices we make, careful money management aims to create a sense of empowerment, reduce stress and promote a healthier relationship with money.

This approach encourages individuals to pay attention to their financial behavior, allowing them to identify patterns, triggers and areas for improvement. Mindful money management is not about deprivation or strict budgeting, but rather about making intentional choices that align with long-term financial well-being. It involves creating a balanced and sustainable financial lifestyle that supports both short-term needs and long-term goals.

Practicing mindfulness in money management means staying present when making financial decisions, whether it's budgeting, investing, or spending. It encourages individuals to explore underlying emotions and beliefs associated with money, such as fear, guilt or abundance. In this way, people can develop a healthier mindset that promotes financial resilience and adaptability in the face of challenges.

One of the key aspects of careful money management is conscious budgeting. Rather than viewing a budget as restrictive, individuals are encouraged to view it as a tool to understand and direct their financial resources. Mindful budgeting involves regularly reviewing your income, expenses, and financial goals and adjusting them as needed to stay aligned with your values and priorities.

In addition to budgeting, mindful money management involves the practice of mindful spending. This means making intentional and conscious decisions about how money will be spent and considering whether purchases align with values and contribute to overall well-being. By cultivating mindfulness in spending, individuals can avoid making impulsive decisions and reduce the likelihood of accumulating unnecessary debt.

Another essential element is careful saving and investing. This includes setting aside money for future goals while being aware of the impact of those choices on current financial well-being.

Mindful investors consider their risk tolerance, long-term goals, and the ethical implications of their investment decisions and tailor their portfolios to their values.

In addition, careful money management goes beyond personal finances to include broader economic and environmental impacts. Conscious consumer choices, ethical investing and the support of sustainable practices are an integral part of this approach. By considering the broader context of financial decisions, individuals can contribute to positive social and environmental outcomes.

Mindful money management is a transformative approach that integrates the principles of mindfulness with practical financial strategies. It enables individuals to develop a deeper understanding of their relationship with money, make intentional choices and create a sustainable financial lifestyle. By cultivating awareness of budgeting, spending, saving and investing, individuals can improve their financial well-being and contribute to a more mindful and sustainable economy.

Chapter 1 Understanding Mindful Money Management in today's world

Mindful money management is a key skill in today's world that goes beyond traditional financial literacy. In a rapidly changing economic environment where financial markets are dynamic and global, understanding the principles of money management is essential for individuals seeking financial well-being and stability.

At its core, mindful money management involves a conscious and intentional approach to managing finances. It goes beyond just budgeting and saving; it includes a holistic understanding of one's financial situation, values and goals. In the context of the modern world, where consumerism and instant gratification often prevail, the adoption of practical money management practices becomes even more relevant.

One of the key aspects of careful money management is creating a comprehensive budget that reflects an individual's income, expenses and savings goals. In today's world dominated by digital transactions, keeping track of all your expenses can be challenging. However, various personal finance apps and tools can help organize and categorize expenses and provide real-time insight into spending.

In addition, careful money management encourages individuals to prioritize their spending based on their values and long-term goals. In a world where trends and fads are constantly influencing consumer behavior, it's easy to succumb to impulse purchases. Being mindful means asking whether a purchase aligns with your values and contributes positively to long-term goals.

In an era of abundant financial resources and information, investing has become an integral part of wealth building strategies. Astute investors consider factors beyond potential returns, such as environmental, social and governance (ESG) criteria. They are aware of the impact their investments can have on society and the environment, and adapt their portfolios to ethical and sustainable principles.

The rise of digital currencies and fintech innovations has also reshaped the field of money management. Mindful individuals are using technology to automate savings, investments and debt repayment, enabling a more efficient and disciplined approach to financial planning. Additionally, staying informed about new financial technologies ensures that individuals can adapt to the evolving financial ecosystem.

Mindful money management goes beyond personal finance; includes an awareness of broader economic trends and global financial issues. In today's connected world, events in distant markets can have a ripple effect on personal finances. Being observant means being informed about economic indicators, geopolitical developments and market trends that can affect financial stability.

A key aspect of careful money management is cultivating a healthy relationship with money. In a society where success is often equated with material wealth, individuals can find themselves trapped in constant comparison and dissatisfaction. Mindfulness promotes a shift in perspective, a focus on gratitude for what one has, and recognition of the intangible aspects of a fulfilling life.

Debt management is another critical component of smart money management, especially in a world where credit is readily available. Considering the consequences of debt, individuals make informed decisions about loans, prioritize debt repayment, and avoid falling into the trap of high-interest loans. This proactive approach contributes to long-term financial health.

The gig economy and telecommuting trends have reshaped the traditional employment landscape. Mindful money management involves adapting to these changes by developing different income streams and maintaining agility in the face of economic uncertainties. Creating an emergency fund becomes essential in a world where job security is less predictable and provides a financial safety net in times of unexpected events.

Understanding how to manage money wisely is more important than ever in today's world. It goes beyond traditional financial practices to include a holistic approach that takes into account values, goals and the wider economic environment. By embracing mindfulness in financial decisions, individuals can navigate the complexities of the modern financial world, build sustainable wealth, and achieve financial well-being.

1.1 Understanding Mindfulness in Finance

Mindfulness in finance goes beyond traditional approaches to money management. It involves the cultivation of increased awareness and conscious presence in financial decision-making, promoting a more holistic and sustainable relationship with money. In the area of careful money management, individuals are encouraged to approach their financial activities with intention, mindfulness and a deep understanding of their financial goals. This article explores the concept of financial mindfulness, its key principles, and its practical applications for achieving a balanced and fulfilling financial life.

1. Awareness of financial behavior:

Mindful money management begins with an acute awareness of your financial behavior. This includes recognizing spending patterns, identifying emotional triggers that lead to impulsive financial decisions, and understanding the impact of those actions on overall financial well-being. By cultivating this awareness, individuals can make more informed and deliberate decisions, aligning their financial behavior with their long-term goals.

2. Engagement in the present moment:

Mindfulness emphasizes the importance of being fully present in the moment. In finance, this means being fully involved in every financial transaction and decision. Instead of dwelling on past financial mistakes or anxiously anticipating future expenses, individuals practicing financial mindfulness focus on the present moment. This not only reduces stress, but also allows for clearer decision-making and the ability to adapt to changing financial situations.

1. Non-Evaluative Observations:

Mindful money management involves observing your financial habits without judgment. Rather than labeling financial behavior as "good" or "bad," individuals practice non-judgmental awareness. This approach allows for a more objective assessment of financial decisions, promotes self-compassion, and creates an environment where individuals can learn from their experiences and make positive changes.

2. Intentional spending:

Mindful spending focuses on intentionality. Before making a purchase, individuals consider whether it aligns with their values and long-term financial goals. This conscious decision-making process minimizes impulse purchases and promotes a more thoughtful relationship with money. By prioritizing needs over wants, individuals can direct their resources toward what is truly important to them.

3. Emotional resilience:

Financial mindfulness equips individuals with the emotional resilience to handle financial challenges. Rather than succumbing to stress or anxiety about money, individuals learn to objectively observe and manage their emotions. This emotional resilience enables them to make sound financial decisions even in the face of uncertainty and promotes long-term financial stability.

Practical Applications of Mindfulness in Finance

1. Smart budgeting:

Traditional budgeting often focuses only on the numbers and overlooks the emotional aspects of spending. On the other hand, careful budgeting involves understanding the emotions and intentions behind each expenditure. By incorporating mindfulness into the budgeting process, individuals can create a more realistic and sustainable financial plan that aligns with their values and priorities.

2. Mindful investing:

Investing with awareness goes beyond the pursuit of short-term gains. It involves a thorough understanding of investment options, considering both financial returns and aligning investments with personal values. Mindful investors stay informed, regularly review their investment portfolios, and make decisions that reflect a long-term vision of financial growth and stability.

3. Cultivating Gratitude for Financial Wellbeing:
Financial mindfulness refers to cultivating gratitude for one's financial well-being. This includes appreciating available resources, acknowledging progress and avoiding the trap of constantly comparing yourself to others. By fostering a sense of gratitude, individuals can develop a healthier relationship with money and reduce the tendency to engage in unnecessary and potentially harmful financial behaviors.

Challenges and Benefits of Mindful Money Management

1. Challenges:

- Overcoming social pressure and consumerism.
- Developing the discipline to consistently practice mindfulness in financial decisions.
- Addressing deep-seated beliefs and attitudes about money.

2. Advantages:
- Better financial decision making.
- Reducing stress and anxiety related to money.
- Increased overall well-being and satisfaction.

Understanding financial mindfulness isn't just about the numbers, it's about developing a deep awareness of our relationship with money. By incorporating mindfulness into financial practices, individuals can overcome a narrow focus on accumulation and spending and develop a more balanced, intentional, and fulfilling approach to managing their finances. Mindful money management is a path that enables individuals to align their financial activities with their values, thereby promoting meaning and satisfaction in their financial lives.

1.2 Importance of Mindful money management

Mindful money management is a crucial aspect of our lives that affects our financial well-being and overall peace of mind. In a time marked by economic uncertainty and a rapidly changing financial environment, the importance of a thoughtful approach to managing our finances cannot be overstated. This article explores the multifaceted importance of careful money management and delves into the benefits it brings to personal finance, mental health, and long-term financial stability.

Understanding Mindful Money Management:
Mindful money management involves a conscious and intentional approach to handling financial resources. It goes beyond just budgeting and tracking expenses and includes a deeper understanding of our financial behavior, values and goals. This approach requires individuals to be fully present and aware of their financial decisions and foster a sense of control and responsibility.

Building financial awareness:

One of the main benefits of careful money management is the cultivation of financial awareness. Many individuals go through life without a clear understanding of their financial situation, leading to overspending, debt accumulation and lack of savings. Mindful money management encourages individuals to regularly assess their financial situation, track expenses and create realistic budgets. This increased awareness enables people to make informed financial decisions and avoid the pitfalls of financial ignorance.

Stress reduction and mental well-being:

Financial stress is a prevalent problem in today's society, affecting individuals at various income levels. Mindful money management acts as a powerful antidote to this stress and promotes mental well-being. When people are mindful of their financial decisions, they can reduce money-related anxiety. The act of consciously planning and managing finances reduces uncertainty and creates a sense of control, which contributes to improved mental health.

Aligning spending with values:
Mindful money management encourages individuals to align their spending with their core values. By identifying and prioritizing what is truly important to them, individuals can make intentional choices that resonate with their personal beliefs and goals. This not only brings a sense of fulfillment, but also prevents mindless spending on items or experiences that do not contribute to long-term happiness.

Creating financial goals:
Setting clear financial goals is the cornerstone of thoughtful money management. Whether it's saving for a house, building an emergency fund, or planning for retirement, well-defined goals give direction and purpose to financial decisions. Mindful individuals carefully consider their short-term and long-term goals and create a plan for achieving financial success.

Developing responsible spending habits:

Mindful money management promotes responsible spending habits by encouraging individuals to question their purchases and assess their true needs. This approach discourages impulsive spending and encourages more thoughtful consideration of financial options. By distinguishing between wants and needs, individuals can reduce unnecessary spending and allocate resources to areas that truly enhance their quality of life.

Building a robust financial foundation:

A key aspect of careful money management is focusing on building a robust financial base. This includes setting up an emergency fund, paying off high-interest debt, and making strategic investments for the future. These essential elements provide financial security and resilience, helping individuals cope with unexpected challenges without compromising their overall financial well-being.

Orientation in economic uncertainties:

In an ever-changing economic environment, it is increasingly important to be mindful of financial decisions. Mindful money management equips individuals with the adaptability needed to overcome economic uncertainties. By being informed, regularly reassessing financial strategies, and being open to adjusting plans when necessary, individuals can better withstand economic fluctuations and ensure financial stability.

Support for long-term financial stability:
Mindful money management is not just about the present; it's about securing a stable financial future. By consistently making informed and intentional financial decisions, individuals lay the foundation for long-term financial stability. This stability provides a sense of confidence and peace of mind knowing that one is well prepared to face future financial challenges.

Supporting sustainable and ethical decisions:
Mindful money management goes beyond personal financial gain; it involves decision-making that is consistent with broader ethical and sustainability

considerations. Individuals who practice careful money management often seek out businesses and investments that prioritize environmental and social responsibility. This not only contributes to a more sustainable world, but also reflects a conscious effort to support ethical practices through financial options.

Strengthening relationships:
Financial matters often play a significant role in relationships, and money-related conflicts can break even the strongest bonds. Mindful money management involves open communication about financial goals, values and spending in relationships. By fostering transparency and understanding, individuals can strengthen their connections and work together toward shared financial goals.

In today's complex and dynamic financial environment, the importance of careful money management cannot be emphasized enough. From building financial awareness and reducing stress to promoting long-term stability and ethical decisions, the benefits of adopting a mindful approach to finances are far-reaching. By incorporating mindfulness into our financial practices, we not only ensure our financial well-being, but also contribute to a more sustainable and fulfilling future.

1.3 How Mindfulness Enhances Financial Well-being

In today's fast-paced world, achieving financial wellness requires more than a robust budget or a savvy investment strategy. The key to long-term financial success lies in the intersection of mindfulness and money management. Mindfulness, often combined with meditation and stress reduction, plays a key role in increasing financial well-being by promoting a deeper understanding of one's financial habits, emotions and decisions.

Understanding Mindfulness in the Context of Finance:
Mindfulness is the practice of being fully present and engaging in the present moment without judgment. When applied to financial matters, it

involves cultivating awareness of our spending patterns, saving habits, and overall financial behavior. Mindful money management encourages individuals to examine their relationship with money, addressing not only the practical aspects of budgeting, but also the emotional and psychological aspects of financial decision-making.

Spending Awareness:
One of the fundamental aspects of careful money management is developing an awareness of spending. Mindfulness encourages individuals to question their purchases and consider whether they align with their values and long-term financial goals. By being aware of every expense, individuals can make more deliberate decisions, avoiding impulsive spending and unnecessary debt.

Emotional intelligence in financial decision-making:
Mindfulness increases emotional intelligence, a key skill in managing finances. It helps individuals recognize and understand their emotions about money, such as anxiety, fear or excitement. By acknowledging these emotions without judgment,

individuals can make more rational and informed financial decisions. This emotional awareness is especially beneficial in times of economic uncertainty and helps individuals navigate financial challenges with resilience.

Breaking the impulse spending cycle:
Mindful money management allows individuals to break out of the cycle of impulsive spending. Through mindfulness practices such as deep breathing or meditation, individuals can develop the ability to stop and think before making impulsive financial decisions. This intentional approach to spending can lead to reduced financial stress and increased satisfaction with your financial choices.

Cultivating a thrifty mindset:
Mindfulness encourages individuals to shift from a scarcity mindset to an abundance mindset, thereby promoting a positive relationship with money. By appreciating the present moment and acknowledging the resources available, individuals are more likely to adopt a proactive approach to saving. Mindful savers typically focus on building an

emergency fund, investing for the future, and achieving financial security.

Reducing financial stress with mindfulness:
Financial stress is a common problem for many individuals and has an impact on both mental and physical well-being. Mindfulness has proven to be an effective tool for reducing stress and promoting overall well-being. By incorporating mindfulness practices into daily life, such as mindful breathing or meditation, individuals can manage financial stress and approach financial decisions with greater clarity and equanimity.

Building long-term financial resilience:
Mindful money management goes beyond short-term financial goals; emphasizes building long-term financial resilience. Through regular mindfulness practices, individuals can develop the discipline to stay focused on their financial goals, resist financial setbacks, and adapt to changing circumstances. This resilience is a key part of lasting financial well-being.

On the road to financial well-being, integrating mindfulness and money management is proving to be a powerful combination. By cultivating awareness, understanding emotions, and making intentional choices, individuals can change their relationship with money. Mindful money management is not a one-size-fits-all solution, but rather a personalized and sustainable approach to achieving lasting financial success. As we navigate the complexities of modern life, the practice of mindfulness offers a transformative path to a healthier and more prosperous financial future.

Chapter 2. Building a Mindful Money Mindset

Building a mindful approach to money is a fundamental aspect of cultivating effective and sustainable financial practices. Mindfulness, a practice rooted in presence and awareness, can significantly affect how we approach, perceive, and manage our money. In this exploration of mindful money management, we'll delve into the basic principles of mindfulness, its application to financial decision-making, and practical steps to developing mindful thinking about money.

Understanding Mindfulness:

Mindfulness is the practice of bringing attention to the present moment without judgment. It involves being fully engaged in the here and now, fostering heightened awareness of thoughts, feelings and surroundings. Applying mindfulness to money management means cultivating a conscious and intentional relationship with our finances.

1. Awareness of financial habits:

Mindfulness forces us to observe our financial behavior without criticism. By understanding our spending, saving and investing habits, we gain insight into the patterns that shape our financial well-being.

2. Emotional Resilience:

Financial decisions often evoke strong emotions. Mindfulness helps in acknowledging these emotions without being overwhelmed, leading to more measured and thoughtful decisions.

3. Reducing Impulsive Spending:

Mindful awareness can reduce impulse spending by encouraging us to stop, think, and question the necessity of a purchase. This deliberative approach helps distinguish between wants and needs.

Basic principles of mindful money management:

1. Gratitude for Finances:

Practice gratitude for your financial situation and become aware of both abundance and scarcity. This change in thinking promotes satisfaction and reduces the constant striving for more.

2. Non-attachment to material possessions:
Mindful money management involves letting go of attachment to material possessions as a source of happiness. Instead, find joy in experiences, relationships, and personal growth.

3. Accepting Financial Reality:
Face your financial situation without judgment. Recognize the challenges, learn from past mistakes, and commit to making positive changes moving forward.

4. **Setting clear financial intentions:**
Define your financial goals and align them with your values. Mindful money management involves purposeful actions that support these intentions.

Practical steps for cultivating mindful thinking about money:

1. Daily Financial Considerations:

Take a few minutes each day to think about your financial decisions. Consider what went well, areas for improvement, and how your decisions align with your financial goals.

2. Mindful Budgeting:

Approach budgeting as a practical exercise. Be present when reviewing your income and expenses and make informed decisions about where your money will go.

3. Regular financial checks:

Schedule regular check-ins to assess your progress toward your financial goals. Use these moments to celebrate accomplishments, adjust strategies, and strengthen your commitment to careful money management.

4. Important Spending:

Before making a purchase, stop and ask yourself if it aligns with your values and financial goals.

Avoid impulsive spending by introducing mindfulness into your consumer decisions.

5. Gratitude Journal for Finances:

Keep a gratitude journal specifically focused on your financial life. Regularly write down aspects of your financial situation that you are grateful for to encourage positive thinking.

Overcoming challenges using conscious approaches:

1. Financial Stress Solutions:

Mindfulness helps manage financial stress by encouraging acceptance of the present moment. Techniques like mindful breathing can provide a sense of calm during challenging times.

2. Financial Failure Solutions:

Rather than dwelling on failures, mindfulness promotes learning from them. Adopt a growth mindset and view challenges as opportunities for personal and financial development.

3. Avoidance of comparison:

Mindful money management involves recognizing that everyone's financial journey is unique. Avoid comparing your situation with others, as this can lead to unnecessary stress and dissatisfaction.

Mindfulness and long-term financial planning:

1. Retirement Planning:

Apply mindfulness to long-term financial planning for the lifestyle you envision during retirement. Reassess your goals regularly and adjust your plan accordingly.

2. Investment Attention:

Approach investments with a careful perspective. Understand the risks, adjust your investments to your values and avoid making decisions based only on short-term market fluctuations.

Cultivating a mindful mindset toward money is an ongoing journey that connects the principles of mindfulness with sound financial practices. By incorporating awareness, intentionality, and gratitude into our financial decisions, we can foster a healthier relationship with money. Remember, the essence of mindful money management is embracing the present moment, learning from the past, and intentionally creating a financially secure and fulfilling future.

2.1 Cultivating Financial Awareness

Financial awareness is the cornerstone of effective money management and, when combined with mindfulness, becomes a powerful tool for achieving financial well-being. In a world driven by consumerism and constant financial pressures, developing a keen understanding of the financial environment is key to making informed decisions and building a secure future.

Understanding Financial Awareness:
Financial awareness goes beyond simply tracking income and expenses; it involves a holistic understanding of one's financial situation. This includes awareness of income sources, spending patterns, savings, investments, debt and financial goals. Developing financial literacy requires a

conscious effort to be informed about personal finances and forms the basis for making sound financial decisions.

Mindful Money Management: The Intersection of Awareness and Intention:

Mindful money management involves applying the principles of mindfulness to financial decisions. Derived from ancient contemplative practices, mindfulness promotes being present and fully engaged in the present moment. When applied to finance, this means making financial decisions consciously and deliberately, without impulsive reactions.

1. Spending Awareness:
Mindful money management starts with being aware of your spending habits. Regularly tracking expenses allows individuals to identify areas where money is being spent impulsively or unnecessarily. By understanding these patterns, deliberate decisions can be made about where to allocate resources.

2. Setting financial goals:

Mindfulness encourages individuals to set clear and realistic financial goals. Whether saving for housing, education or retirement, setting Specific, Measurable, Attainable, Relevant and Time-bound (SMART) goals provides a blueprint for financial success. Careful goal setting ensures that financial goals are aligned with personal values and aspirations.

3. Budgeting with intention:

Budgeting is a fundamental aspect of managing money, but doing it mindfully adds another layer of intentionality. Mindful budgeting involves allocating resources based on priorities and values. It requires regular review of the budget to ensure that it is consistent with the current financial situation and goals.

Benefits of Cultivating Financial Awareness Through Mindful Money Management

1. Reducing financial stress:

Understanding your financial situation and actively managing your money with mindfulness can significantly reduce financial stress. The awareness that comes with conscious money management allows individuals to make informed decisions and promotes a sense of control over their financial destiny.

2. Improved financial decision making:
Financial awareness strengthens decision-making. By knowing their income, expenses and financial goals, individuals can make informed decisions about spending, saving and investing. This leads to a more efficient allocation of resources, leading to financial growth and stability.

3. Improved Savings and Investing:
Mindful money management supports disciplined saving and investing. With a clear understanding of financial goals and a mindful approach to spending, individuals are better positioned to allocate funds to both short-term and long-term goals. This in turn helps build wealth over time.

4. Increased financial resilience:

Financial awareness promotes resilience to economic uncertainties. Mindful individuals are more likely to have emergency funds, diversified investments, and a strategic approach to debt management. This resilience provides a buffer against unexpected financial problems.

5. Aligning finances with values:

Mindful money management allows individuals to align their financial decisions with their values. This alignment not only contributes to personal satisfaction, but also helps build a financial life that reflects one's core principles and desires.

Practical Steps to Cultivating Financial Awareness

1. Track income and expenses regularly:

Maintain detailed records of income and expenses to understand spending patterns and identify areas for improvement.

2. Set clear financial goals:

Define short-term and long-term financial goals that are specific, measurable, achievable, relevant and time-bound (SMART).

3. Create and regularly review budgets:
Develop a budget that reflects financial goals and regularly review and adjust it to reflect changes in income, expenses, and goals.

4. Create an emergency fund:
Set aside funds for unexpected expenses to create a financial safety net.

5. Educate yourself:
Stay informed about financial matters, including investments, taxes and personal finance principles. Continuing education increases financial awareness.

6. Request expert advice:
Consultations with financial advisors can provide valuable insights and advice tailored to individual circumstances.

Cultivating financial literacy through mindful money management is an ongoing process that empowers individuals to take control of their financial destinies. By combining an understanding of financial fundamentals with an intentional, present-centered approach to mindfulness, individuals can make informed decisions, reduce financial stress, and build a path to financial wellness. It's not just about the numbers; it's about creating a financial life that aligns with personal values and aspirations, fostering a sense of security and satisfaction on the path to financial success.

2.3 Mindful Spending Habits

Mindful spending plays a key role in the broader spectrum of mindful money management. In a world dominated by consumerism, where temptations to spend abound, cultivating mindfulness in financial decisions becomes essential to achieving long-term financial well-being.

At its core, mindful spending involves a conscious awareness of your financial choices and their impact on your overall financial health. It goes beyond the mere act of budgeting and delves into the psychological and emotional aspects of managing money. Here we explore the principles and benefits of mindful spending habits and their deep connection to holistic money management.

Understanding Mindful Spending:
Mindful spending is rooted in the idea of intentional choices. It encourages individuals to consider their values, needs and long-term goals before making any purchase. This process involves pausing to reflect on whether a particular expenditure aligns with their values and makes a positive contribution to their lives.

For example, someone who practices mindful spending might question whether buying the latest gadget is in line with their goal of saving for housing or investing in education. By being aware of these choices, individuals can make choices that promote financial stability and align with their overarching life goals.

The Psychology of Mindful Spending:

To understand the importance of mindful spending, we need to delve into the psychology of consumer behavior. A fast-paced, consumer-driven society often encourages impulse purchases and instant gratification. However, mindful spending promotes a shift from reactive to proactive financial decision-making.

Through mindfulness, individuals become aware of the emotional triggers that lead to unnecessary purchases. Whether it's a desire for status, a need for comfort, or succumbing to marketing tactics, mindfulness allows you to step back and objectively evaluate these triggers. This heightened awareness allows individuals to make decisions based on real needs rather than fleeting impulses.

Budget with purpose:

Mindful spending is intricately linked to purposeful budgeting. Rather than viewing a budget as a restrictive tool, frugal individuals see it as a guiding framework aligned with their values. Budgets become a means of purposefully allocating resources, ensuring that every dollar spent contributes to personal fulfillment and financial goals.

In addition, careful budgeting encourages regular reviews and adjustments. As circumstances change, so do financial priorities. Regularly reviewing and adjusting your budget ensures that it remains a dynamic tool that adapts to life's changing demands while staying in line with your financial aspirations.

Cultivating Contentment:

Mindful spending promotes a shift from a mindset of constant wanting to one of contentment. This shift is especially important in a culture that often equates happiness with material possessions. Mindfulness encourages individuals to find joy in experiences, relationships, and personal growth, promoting contentment that goes beyond material accumulation.

By recognizing and appreciating what you already have, the allure of unnecessary purchases diminishes. This newfound contentment not only contributes to financial well-being, but also increases overall life satisfaction.

Building resilience and preparedness:

Mindful spending is an integral part of building financial resilience. By making deliberate decisions and prioritizing needs over wants, individuals build a financial cushion that can withstand unexpected challenges. Whether it's a medical emergency, job loss, or economic downturn, the principles of mindful money management equip individuals with the resilience needed to overcome unforeseen circumstances.

In addition, frugal spending helps build emergency funds and savings. These financial buffers act as safety nets that provide a sense of security and peace of mind in the face of uncertainties.

Impact on the environment and society:

Beyond the personal benefits, conscious spending extends its impact to the wider social and environmental context. By considering the ethical and environmental implications of purchases, individuals contribute to a more sustainable and socially responsible economy. Mindful consumers support businesses that are aligned with their values, fostering a positive cycle that promotes ethical practices and environmental responsibility.

Mindful spending is not just about cutting expenses or sticking to a strict budget. They embody a holistic approach to money management that connects financial decisions with values, goals and overall well-being. Through intentional choices, a shift in thinking, and a commitment to financial mindfulness, individuals can pave the way to a secure and fulfilling financial future.

By understanding the complex connection between mindful spending and money management, individuals gain tools to navigate the complexities of personal finance with clarity and purpose. In a world where financial decisions can often be overwhelming, adopting mindfulness becomes a guiding light that illuminates the path to a balanced and prosperous financial life.

2.4 Developing a Positive Relationship with Money

Money is a pervasive aspect of our lives, influencing our choices, opportunities and even our well-being. Yet many individuals' relationship with money is often fraught with stress, anxiety and uncertainty. If you want to cultivate a positive relationship with money, it is essential to learn practical money management practices. This involves a holistic approach that goes beyond simple budgeting and saving, delving into the psychological and emotional aspects of our financial behavior.

Understanding your money mindset:

To foster a positive relationship with money, you must first understand their money mindset. It is a set of beliefs and attitudes that shape the way an individual approaches and interacts with money. It is often formed in childhood by observing family members, experiences and social influences.

Thinking about your money mindset will allow you to identify any negative beliefs or patterns that may be hindering your financial well-being. Whether it's the fear of lack, the guilt associated with spending, or the belief that money is inherently evil, recognizing these attitudes is the first step to transformation.

Adopting mindfulness when making financial decisions:

Mindful money management means being fully present and aware of your financial possibilities. Instead of making impulsive decisions driven by fear or desire, take the time to consider the long-term consequences of your actions. This can include asking if the purchase aligns with your values, assessing the impact on your financial goals, and understanding the emotions that drive your financial decisions.

Practicing mindfulness in financial decision-making helps break the cycle of reactive spending and encourages intentional decisions that contribute to your overall well-being. It's about aligning your financial habits with your values and long-term aspirations.

Creating a holistic budget:

While budgeting is a fundamental aspect of managing money, a thoughtful approach involves creating a holistic budget that takes into account not only expenses, but also your values and priorities. Start by categorizing your expenses into essentials, nonessentials, and savings. This allows you to see where your money is going and identify areas for potential adjustments.

Allocate resources based on your values. If health and well-being are important to you, prioritize spending on activities that contribute to your physical and mental well-being. Aligning your budget with your values will ensure that your money serves your overall life goals, leading to a more positive and meaningful financial existence.

Practicing gratitude for financial abundance:

A positive relationship with money involves acknowledging and appreciating the financial resources you have. Practicing gratitude for what you already have can shift your focus from scarcity to abundance. Take time to regularly think about the financial aspects of your life that bring you joy, security, or fulfillment.

Expressing gratitude can be as simple as acknowledging the stability of a roof over your head, the ability to afford nutritious food, or the opportunities that financial resources provide. By cultivating an attitude of gratitude, you shift your mindset from scarcity to abundance, fostering a more positive and powerful relationship with money.

Creating an emergency fund for financial security:
Mindful money management involves preparing for the unexpected. Creating an emergency fund is an essential step to creating financial security and peace of mind. This fund serves as a buffer against unexpected expenses, helping you navigate life's uncertainties without jeopardizing your financial stability.

Contribute regularly to your emergency fund and consider it a non-negotiable expense in your budget. Knowing you have a financial safety net allows you to face challenges with resilience and reduces the stress of unexpected financial setbacks.

Cultivating long-term financial goals:
A positive relationship with money is not just about managing your daily expenses; it is also about planning for the future. Cultivate long-term financial goals that align with your aspirations and values.

Whether it's saving for a home, funding education, or planning for retirement, clear goals provide meaning and direction.

Break these goals down into manageable steps and celebrate small successes along the way. This approach encourages positive thinking by focusing on progress rather than distance to cover. Revisit and adjust your goals regularly as your life circumstances evolve to ensure they remain aligned with your values.

Seek professional help if necessary:

Developing a positive relationship with money is not just about overcoming financial problems. Seeking professional advice, such as working with a financial planner or advisor, can provide valuable insight and support. These experts can offer personalized strategies to help you make informed decisions and navigate complex financial environments.

Additionally, discussing financial matters with a trusted friend or family member can offer different perspectives and emotional support. Breaking the taboo around money conversations can lead to a healthier relationship with finances and foster a sense of community around shared financial goals.

Developing a positive relationship with money through careful money management is a transformational journey that goes beyond traditional budgeting techniques. By understanding and reshaping your thinking about money, embracing mindfulness in your financial decision-making, and aligning your spending with your values, you can develop a more meaningful and powerful relationship with money.

Remember, it's not just about accumulating wealth; it's about using your financial resources to create a life that aligns with your values and brings fulfillment. With practices like gratitude, building an emergency fund, setting long-term goals, and seeking professional guidance when needed, you can navigate the complexities of personal finance with confidence and positivity.

Chapter3. Practical Strategies for Mindful Budgeting

Mindful budgeting is a holistic approach to managing your finances that goes beyond just crunching the numbers. It involves cultivating awareness and intentionality in your financial decisions, aligning your spending with your values, and fostering a healthy relationship with money. In this article, we'll explore practical strategies for mindful budgeting that will put you in control of your financial well-being.

1. Understand Your Financial Environment:
   - Start by getting a comprehensive overview of your financial situation. List all sources of income, monthly expenses, debts and savings. This awareness forms the basis of thoughtful budgeting.

2. Set clear financial goals:

- Set short-term and long-term financial goals. Whether it's saving for a vacation, an emergency fund, or retirement, clear goals provide direction for your budgeting efforts.

3. Create a realistic budget:

- Create a budget that reflects your financial reality. Divide expenses into fixed (eg rent, energy) and variable (eg food, entertainment). Be realistic about your spending habits to create a budget that is sustainable.

4. Prioritize essential expenses:

- Identify non-negotiable expenses such as housing, utilities and food. Make sure these essentials are prioritized in your budget, allowing you to cover basic needs before allocating funds for discretionary spending.

5. Embrace Mindful Spending:

- Cultivate awareness of your spending habits. Before making a purchase, ask yourself if it aligns with your values and goals. Mindful spending involves making intentional choices that contribute to your overall well-being.

6. Track Your Spending:

- Track and control your expenses regularly. Use budgeting apps or spreadsheets to track transactions. This practice increases awareness of your financial habits and helps identify areas for improvement.

7. Build an Emergency Fund:

- Allocate a portion of your income to an emergency fund. Having a financial safety net provides peace of mind and prevents the need to dip into long-term savings or take on high-interest debt in the event of an unexpected expense.

8. Automate Savings:

- Simplify the savings process by automating transfers to your savings account. This ensures that you are consistently contributing to your financial goals without being tempted to spend money elsewhere.

9. Expense Negotiation:

- Regularly review accounts and negotiate where possible. This includes utilities, insurance and subscriptions. Negotiations can lead to reduced expenses and freeing up funds for other financial goals.

10. Debt Repayment Strategy:

- Develop a strategic debt repayment plan. Consider prioritizing high-interest debt first, using methods such as a debt avalanche or debt snowball to speed up the repayment process.

11. Invest in Financial Education:

- Increase your financial literacy by investing time in learning about personal finance. Understanding concepts like investing, taxes, and retirement planning allows you to make informed decisions.

12. Practice Gratitude:

- Cultivate a mindset of gratitude for your current financial situation. This doesn't mean ignoring challenges, but rather acknowledging the progress you've made and maintaining a positive outlook on your financial journey.

13. Regularly check and adjust:

  - Financial situations change and so should your budget. Review your budget regularly to make sure it fits your current situation and adjust it as needed. This adaptability is critical to long-term success.

14. Seek professional advice:

  - If necessary, consult financial advisors or experts and get personalized advice. Professionals can offer you information tailored to your specific financial goals and circumstances.

Mindful budgeting is a dynamic process that involves constant self-reflection and adaptation. By understanding your financial environment, setting clear goals and implementing practical strategies, you can foster a mindful approach to money management. Remember, it's not just about the numbers on the table; it's about creating a sustainable and fulfilling financial life that aligns with your values.

3.1 Creating a Mindful Budget

Creating a conscious budget is a fundamental aspect of practical money management. In a world of financial stress, a mindful approach to budgeting can lead to increased financial well-being and peace of mind. This holistic view of budgeting goes beyond mere numbers to include a conscious awareness of one's financial capabilities, values and overall lifestyle. Let's dive into the key components of mindful budgeting and explore how it contributes to a more mindful approach to money.

Understanding Mindful Money Management:
Mindful money management involves full presence and awareness when making financial decisions. It's about cultivating an awareness of your spending habits, values, and long-term financial goals. By incorporating mindfulness into your budgeting process, you can gain a deeper understanding of your relationship with money and make intentional decisions that align with your values.

Setting Conscious Financial Goals:

The first step in creating a thoughtful budget is setting clear and realistic financial goals. These goals should reflect your values and priorities, whether they include saving for that dream vacation, building an emergency fund, or paying off debt. Mindful financial goals provide a sense of purpose, guide your budgeting decisions, and encourage thoughtful spending.

Conscious Spending:

Mindful budgeting promotes conscious spending by promoting awareness of where your money is going. Track and review your spending regularly to identify patterns and areas for improvement. Ask yourself if your spending is in line with your priorities and values. This level of awareness can lead to informed decisions, helping you cut unnecessary expenses and redirect funds to your financial goals.

Mindful Storage:

Saving money involves more than just putting away a fixed amount each month. It requires understanding the purpose of your savings and intentionally building financial security. Whether you're saving for a specific goal or building an emergency fund, allocate wisely and consider the long-term impact of your savings habits on your overall financial well-being.

Embracing Simplicity:

A mindful budget often emphasizes simplicity and minimalism. Simplifying your lifestyle and spending can lead to financial freedom and reduced stress. Evaluate your possessions and spending options and focus on what really adds value to your life. This mindful approach can lead to more intentional and fulfilling spending and avoid the trap of consumerism and impulse buying.

Gratitude Exercise:

Mindful money management involves cultivating gratitude for your financial resources. Regularly express appreciation for the income you earn, the ability to meet your basic needs, and the opportunity to work toward your financial goals. Gratitude can shift your mindset from scarcity to abundance, fostering a positive relationship with money and reducing the temptation to overspend.

Conscious Decision Making:
Conscious decision-making is at the heart of thoughtful budgeting. Before making any financial decision, take a moment to think about your values, priorities, and long-term goals. Mindful decision-making involves considering the impact of your decisions on your overall well-being and financial future. This intentional approach can prevent impulsive decisions and promote financial stability.

Creating an Emergency Fund:
A careful budget includes reserves for unexpected expenses. Building an emergency fund is an integral part of careful money management and provides a financial safety net during challenging times. Prioritize allocating a portion of your income to an emergency fund and realize that it is a key part of your overall financial well-being.

Cultivating Mindful Habits:

Creating a conscious budget is not a one-time task; it's an ongoing process that involves cultivating conscious financial habits. Review your budget regularly, reevaluate your financial goals, and adjust your spending habits as needed. By consistently practicing mindfulness in your financial decisions, you can adapt to changing circumstances and stay on track to achieve your long-term goals.

Mindful Budgeting for Financial Freedom:
Creating a mindful budget is a transformative path to financial freedom and well-being. It goes beyond the traditional concept of budgeting and includes a holistic approach that takes into account your values, goals and overall lifestyle. By incorporating mindfulness into your financial decisions, you can cultivate a healthy relationship with money, reduce financial stress, and work towards a more fulfilling and prosperous future.

3.2 Tracking Expenses Mindfully

Keeping a close watch on expenses is a crucial aspect of careful money management, fostering a deeper understanding of financial habits and promoting responsible spending. In this comprehensive guide, we'll explore the importance of tracking your spending, delve into practical strategies for keeping a close eye, and highlight the transformative impact it can have on your overall financial well-being.

Understanding Mindful Money Management:

Mindful money management involves cultivating a conscious awareness of your financial decisions, values, and goals. It goes beyond mere budgeting and transcends the traditional approach to finance. Central to this philosophy is the concept of mindfulness – a state of being fully present and engaged in the present moment. Practicing mindfulness when managing money means being aware of your financial options, understanding their motivations, and making decisions that align with your values.

The Importance of Closely Tracking Your Expenses

1. Looking into Spending Patterns:

Closely monitoring your expenses provides a detailed view of your spending patterns. By carefully recording every transaction, you'll gain insight into where your money is going, allowing you to identify areas where you can cut back or reallocate funds.

2. Adjustment of budget:

It allows you to match your expenses with your budget. Close monitoring ensures that you stay within your allocated limits for different spending categories, prevent overspending and promote financial discipline.

3. Identification of financial goals:

Tracking expenses consciously makes it easier to identify short-term and long-term financial goals. Whether it's saving for a vacation, an emergency fund, or retirement, understanding your spending habits will help you allocate funds appropriately.

4. Reducing Financial Stress:

Knowing exactly where your money is going reduces financial uncertainty and stress. Keeping a close eye on your expenses allows you to face your financial situation clearly, making it easier to deal with challenges and plan for the future.

Practical Strategies for Mindful Spending Tracking

1. Create a detailed budget:

Start by creating a comprehensive budget that includes all sources of income and anticipated expenses. Allocate specific amounts to categories such as housing, groceries, utilities, entertainment, and savings.

2. Use technology to your advantage:

Use personal finance apps or budgeting tools to streamline the tracking process. These tools often sync with bank accounts and credit cards, automatically categorizing transactions and providing real-time insight into your financial situation.

3. Regularly check and adjust:

Set aside time each week or month to review your expenses. Analyze your transactions, compare them to your budget, and make adjustments as needed. This ongoing process ensures that your financial plan remains dynamic and responsive to changes in your life.

4. Accept Cash Transactions:

For certain budget categories, consider using cash instead of cards. Cash transactions are tangible and create an increased awareness of your spending, encouraging mindfulness in your everyday purchases.

5. Categorization and Prioritization:

Categorize your expenses to better understand where your money is going. Prioritize essential expenses and allocate discretionary expenses based on your values and financial goals.

Transformative impact on financial well-being

1. Increased financial awareness:

Careful monitoring of expenses promotes increased financial awareness. This awareness goes beyond numbers to include the emotions and motivations behind your spending decisions.

2. Improved Decision Making:

Armed with a clear understanding of your financial situation, you can make informed decisions. Whether it's adjusting your budget, cutting unnecessary expenses, or redirecting funds to savings, careful monitoring will allow you to take control of your financial destiny.

3. Building Healthy Financial Habits:

Consistent monitoring cultivates healthy financial habits. Over time, managing your money wisely becomes second nature, leading to sustainable practices that support your overall financial well-being.

4. Achieving financial goals:

Mindful monitoring is a tool to achieve financial goals. Whether it's building an emergency fund, paying off debt, or saving for a big purchase, the discipline cultivated through tracking your spending will propel you toward success.

Overcoming challenges while keeping a close eye on spending

1. Consistency is key:

One of the challenges of keeping a close eye on spending is maintaining consistency. Establishing a routine and incorporating tracking into your daily or weekly habits helps overcome this obstacle.

2. Dealing with Emotional Spending:

Mindful tracking reveals the emotional triggers that lead to impulsive spending. Addressing the emotional aspects of financial decisions is essential to developing a healthy relationship with money.

3. Adapting to Change:

Life is dynamic and your financial situation can change. Adapting your tracking methods to these changes will ensure your money management remains efficient and relevant.

Careful monitoring of expenses is a transformative practice that is in line with the principles of prudent money management. It provides invaluable insights, promotes responsible financial habits, and empowers individuals to make informed decisions that lead to a secure and fulfilling financial future. By incorporating mindfulness into personal finance, individuals can embark on a path to financial well-being and achieve a harmonious balance between their financial goals and the present moment.

3.3 Prioritizing Spending Based on Values

In today's fast-paced world, managing your finances can often seem like a daunting task. From bills to everyday expenses, the demands on our wallets can be overwhelming. However, adopting a mindful approach to money management can bring clarity and purpose to your financial decisions. One of the key aspects of careful money management is prioritizing your spending based on your values.

Understanding Mindful Money Management:

Mindful money management involves being conscious and intentional about how you earn, spend, and save money. It's about aligning your financial decisions with your values, goals and aspirations. This will create a harmonious relationship with your money and promote a sense of control and contentment.

Identifying your core values:

The first step in prioritizing values-based spending is identifying your core values. These are the principles and beliefs that matter most to you. Your values may include things like family, education, health, adventure, or community. Take the time to think about what is really important to you, both short and long term.

Creating a values-based budget:

Once you've determined your core values, it's time to create a values-based budget. This includes allocating your income to match your values. For example, if health is a priority, you can set aside a portion of your budget for gym memberships, nutritious food, or wellness activities. If education is important, you can set aside funds for courses, workshops or books.

Impact on daily expenses:
Prioritizing spending based on values has a profound impact on your everyday financial decisions. Instead of mindlessly spending on impulse purchases, you'll find yourself making choices that contribute to your overall well-being and fulfillment. It's not about depriving yourself of pleasure, but rather making sure your spending aligns with your values.

Building an emergency fund:
In the area of careful money management, building an emergency fund is a crucial step. This financial cushion provides peace of mind and stability during unexpected events. Whether it's a medical emergency or a sudden repair, having an emergency fund is in line with the value of preparedness and safety.

Invest in experiences before possessions:

In a consumerist society, it is easy to fall into the trap of accumulating possessions. Careful money management, however, encourages investing in experiences over possessions. Experiences such as travel, cultural events or educational opportunities often provide more lasting satisfaction and are aligned with values such as personal growth and enjoyment.

Say no to the inflation lifestyle:
As your income increases, it can be tempting to indulge in lifestyle inflation – upgrading your car, living space or wardrobe. Mindful money management invites you to question whether these choices align with your values or are simply driven by societal expectations. Saying no to unnecessary lifestyle inflation allows you to allocate resources where they really matter.

The role of mindfulness in financial decisions:
Mindfulness plays a vital role in making intentional financial decisions. By staying present and aware, you can avoid impulsive spending and stay true to your values. Before making a purchase, take a

moment to think about whether it aligns with your priorities. This pause can make a big difference in directing your money to what really matters.

Overcoming challenges:
While values-based spending prioritization is an effective approach, it is not without challenges. Barriers can be peer pressure, societal expectations, and the lure of instant gratification. Overcoming these challenges requires a commitment to your values and a strong sense of self-awareness. Regularly reassessing your financial decisions will ensure they remain aligned with your evolving values.

Learning to manage money wisely for others:
The benefits of careful money management go beyond personal satisfaction. Sharing these principles with family, friends or colleagues can create a ripple effect of positive financial habits. Workshops, discussions or simply leading by example can contribute to a collective shift towards more considerate, values-based financial practices.

In personal finance, prioritizing spending based on values is a transformative approach. It goes beyond traditional notions of budgeting and brings deeper meaning to your financial decisions. By aligning your money with your values, you will not only foster a healthier relationship with your finances, but also contribute to a more meaningful and fulfilling life. Mindful money management isn't just about dollars and cents; it's about creating a life that reflects what really matters to you.

3.4 Adapting Budgets for Changing Circumstances

The only constant in personal finance is change. The unpredictable nature of life often throws unexpected challenges our way, so adopting a flexible and considerate approach to budgeting is essential. Adapting budgets to changing circumstances is not only a practical necessity, but also a key part of conscious money management.

Understanding the Dynamic Nature of Life:

Life is a dynamic journey with its fair share of ups and downs. Whether it's a sudden job loss, unexpected medical expenses, or a major life event like getting married or having children, our financial situation is constantly changing. This dynamic requires a budgeting strategy that can evolve with our lives.

Basics of Mindful Money Management:
Mindful money management involves being fully aware of your financial situation, making intentional decisions, and adapting to change with a sense of awareness. At the heart of this approach is the understanding that a budget is not a fixed set of rules, but a dynamic tool that should fit your current needs and circumstances.

Creating a flexible budget framework:
To embrace frugal money management, start by creating a flexible budget framework. Instead of sticking to fixed categories and amounts, allocate a portion of your budget to "flexible spending." This may include unexpected expenses or adjustments necessary due to changes in income. By allowing

for this flexibility, you will be better prepared to handle the inevitable twists and turns that life throws at you.

Emergency Fund: The Foundation for Financial Resilience:

Building an emergency fund into your budget is a cornerstone of smart money management. This financial safety net provides a cushion during challenging times, offering peace of mind and the ability to adapt to unexpected circumstances without jeopardizing your overall financial stability. Aim to save three to six months of living expenses in your emergency fund.

Regular review and adjustment of budgets:

A budget is not a one-size-fits-all solution. It is a dynamic tool that requires regular review and adjustments. Schedule regular financial reviews to evaluate the effectiveness of your budget and make necessary adjustments. This proactive approach ensures that your budget stays in line with your financial goals and adapts to the evolving circumstances of your life.

Prioritizing spending: needs vs. washings:

Mindful money management involves distinguishing between needs and wants. During times of change, prioritize spending on basic needs such as housing, utilities and food. This ensures that the essential elements of your well-being are protected, even if you need to make adjustments in other areas.

Negotiating Fixed Expenses:

Fixed expenses such as rent or mortgage payments may seem inflexible, but there is often room for negotiation. In times of financial distress, explore options for renegotiating contracts or consolidating debt. Many service providers are willing to work with individuals who are facing challenges, especially if it means maintaining a long-term relationship.

Leveraging Technology for Adaptive Budgeting:

In the digital age, many apps and tools can help with adaptive budgeting. Use budgeting apps that allow you to track your expenses in real time and provide insight into your financial health. These tools allow you to make informed decisions quickly and ensure your budget remains resilient to changing circumstances.

Seeking Professional Advice:
When going through significant financial changes, seeking professional advice can be invaluable. Financial advisors can offer personalized insights to help you make informed decisions about your budget, investments and overall financial strategy. Their expertise can provide a strategic perspective that will enhance your ability to adapt to changing circumstances.

Cultivating a Conscious Financial Mindset:
Mindful money management goes beyond budgeting; it involves cultivating a conscious financial mindset. This mindset promotes gratitude for what you have, a conscious awareness of your financial options, and an understanding that adaptability is a strength, not a weakness. Adopting a mindful approach to finances promotes resilience and helps you navigate life's uncertainties more easily.

Adapting budgets to changing circumstances is a fundamental aspect of sound money management. By recognizing the dynamic nature of life, creating flexible budget frameworks, prioritizing needs, and using tools and professional advice, you can build financial resilience. Cultivating a mindful financial mindset ensures that your approach to money management aligns with your values and allows you to thrive regardless of life's unpredictable twists and turns.

Chapter 4. Investing with Mindfulness

Mindful investing involves cultivating awareness and intentionality in financial decisions. Mindful money management goes beyond mere numbers and focuses on the holistic well-being of individuals and society. In this comprehensive survey, we dive into the principles of mindful investing and how it intersects with careful money management.

Understanding Mindfulness in Investing:
Rooted in ancient contemplative practices, mindfulness encourages individuals to be present and fully engaged in the present moment. Applied to investing, this means being aware of your financial goals, risk tolerance, and the broader impact of your decisions. Mindful investors take a deliberate approach, taking into account not only

the potential returns, but also the ethical and environmental implications of their investments.

The intersection of mindfulness and financial goals:
Mindful money management starts with clarifying your financial goals. Investors are encouraged to think about what's really important to them, whether that's saving for retirement, supporting a sustainable business or contributing to social causes. This introspective process allows investors to align their financial strategies with their values, thereby supporting the meaning of their investment journey.

Conscious investment strategies:

1. Socially Responsible Investing (SRI): Mindful investors often use SRI and select investments based not only on financial performance but also on environmental, social and governance (ESG) criteria. This approach aligns investment portfolios with ethical values and supports companies

committed to positive social and environmental practices.

2. Impact Investing: Taking mindfulness a step further, impact investors actively seek opportunities to create positive social or environmental impact along with financial return. This may include investments in renewable energy projects, affordable housing initiatives or social justice companies.

Be aware of the risks:

Astute investors recognize the risks associated with financial markets, but approach them with a balanced perspective. Rather than being driven solely by fear or greed, they cultivate a sense of equanimity—peace of mind, especially in challenging market conditions. This way of thinking helps prevent impulsive decisions caused by short-term fluctuations and promotes a more stable and sustainable investment approach.

Emotional intelligence in financial decision-making:

Mindful money management emphasizes emotional intelligence in dealing with financial ups and downs. It encourages investors to recognize and understand their emotions and avoid impulsive reactions during market volatility. When investors stay grounded and make decisions based on thoughtful analysis of information, they can more effectively navigate market fluctuations.

The role of mindfulness in long-term investing:
Mindfulness supports a long-term perspective in investing. Instead of chasing short-term gains, investors focus on building a resilient and diversified portfolio that can weather market fluctuations over time. This patient approach is in line with the principles of conscious living, promoting a sense of contentment and satisfaction with the investment journey.

Integrating Mindfulness Practice:
Mindful money management goes beyond investment decisions and includes everyday financial habits. Integrating mindfulness practices such as careful budgeting, tracking expenses, and

regularly reviewing financial goals helps individuals maintain a conscious and sustainable approach to overall financial well-being.

Overcoming behavioral biases:
Mindful investors actively work to overcome common behavioral biases that can lead to irrational financial decisions. By remaining attuned to their thoughts and feelings about money, they can counter biases such as loss aversion, overconfidence, and recency bias, and foster a more rational and disciplined investment approach.

Mindfulness and financial education:
Promoting financial literacy and mindfulness go hand in hand. Educating individuals about the principles of careful money management enables them to make informed and conscious financial decisions. This includes understanding investment options, risk management and the impact of financial decisions on a personal and societal level.

Investing with awareness is a transformative approach that transcends traditional financial paradigms. It's a path that combines self-awareness, ethical considerations, and a long-term perspective to create a more intentional and fulfilling relationship with money. As we navigate the complex landscape of financial markets, integrating mindfulness into our investment practices can contribute not only to personal financial success, but also to a more sustainable and compassionate global economy.

4.1 Mindful Investment Principles

Mindful investment principles form the cornerstone of a balanced and sustainable approach to managing finances. In an era dominated by fast-paced markets and impulsive decision-making, incorporating mindfulness into investment strategies can lead to more informed choices and long-term financial well-being.

At its core, mindful investing involves cultivating an awareness of one's financial goals, risk tolerance, and the broader economic landscape. This awareness extends beyond mere numbers on a balance sheet; it encompasses a holistic understanding of the psychological, emotional, and societal factors influencing financial decisions.

To begin with, one of the fundamental principles of mindful investing is setting clear and realistic financial goals. Mindful investors take the time to reflect on what they want to achieve – whether it's funding their children's education, buying a home, or securing a comfortable retirement. By establishing concrete objectives, individuals can align their investment strategies with their broader life aspirations.

Furthermore, mindful investors prioritize understanding their risk tolerance. Rather than succumbing to market fluctuations and short-term volatility, they assess their ability to weather financial storms and make investment choices that align with their comfort levels. This self-awareness acts as a safeguard against impulsive decisions, fostering a sense of calm and resilience during turbulent market conditions.

In addition to self-awareness, mindful investment involves staying well-informed about the broader economic landscape. This includes keeping abreast of geopolitical events, economic indicators, and market trends. By staying informed, investors can make decisions based on a comprehensive understanding of the factors that impact their portfolios. Mindful investors also recognize the importance of continuous learning, adapting to the evolving financial landscape with curiosity and an open mind.

Mindful money management goes beyond the individual level; it extends to the broader societal impact of investments. Ethical considerations play a crucial role in mindful investing, prompting individuals to examine the environmental, social, and governance (ESG) aspects of their portfolios. Investing in companies that align with one's values contributes to a more sustainable and responsible approach to wealth creation.

Another key principle of mindful investing is maintaining a long-term perspective. In a world driven by instant gratification, the ability to resist the allure of quick gains and focus on the enduring value of investments is a hallmark of mindful money management. Patience becomes a virtue as investors ride out market fluctuations, secure in the knowledge that their choices are grounded in a comprehensive understanding of their financial goals.

Mindful investors also emphasize the importance of diversification. By spreading investments across different asset classes, geographic regions, and industries, they reduce the risk associated with over-reliance on a single investment. Diversification acts as a protective shield, ensuring that the impact of a downturn in one sector is mitigated by positive performance in others.

Furthermore, mindful investing involves periodic reassessment of one's portfolio. As financial goals evolve and market conditions change, a thoughtful review of investments ensures that they remain aligned with the investor's objectives. This ongoing evaluation allows for adjustments, rebalancing, and the incorporation of new opportunities that may arise.

Risk management is another critical aspect of mindful money management. Mindful investors recognize that all investments carry some degree of risk, and they employ strategies to mitigate these risks. This may involve setting stop-loss orders, regularly reviewing asset allocations, and staying vigilant to potential shifts in market dynamics.

Mindful investment principles offer a strategic and holistic approach to managing finances. By cultivating self-awareness, staying informed, and considering the broader societal impact of investments, individuals can navigate the complex world of finance with clarity and purpose. Through setting realistic goals, understanding risk tolerance, prioritizing ethical considerations, and maintaining a long-term perspective, mindful investors pave the way for financial well-being and resilience in an ever-changing economic landscape.

4.2 Aligning Investments with Values

In the rapidly developing world of finance, where discussions are dominated by market trends and economic indicators, the concept of aligning investments with personal values is coming to the fore. Mindful money management goes beyond the traditional focus on returns and risks; emphasizes the importance of aligning financial decisions with individual values, ethics and long-term goals. This holistic approach to investing not only contributes to a more sustainable and responsible financial environment, but also provides investors with a sense of purpose and fulfillment. In this comprehensive guide, we explore the principles, benefits and practical steps of aligning investing with values for those seeking a more mindful approach to wealth creation.

Understanding Mindful Money Management:
Mindful money management involves a conscious and intentional effort to integrate personal values into financial decision-making. Investors are increasingly aware of the impact their capital can have on social and environmental issues. By aligning investments with values, individuals strive to create a positive impact on the world while achieving financial goals.

Principles of aligning investments with values:

1. Determination of basic values:

In order to align investments with values, it is important to first identify your core values. These may include environmental sustainability, social justice, corporate governance or ethical business practices. Understanding these values provides the basis for informed investment decisions.

2. Environmental, Social and Governance (ESG) criteria:

Integrating ESG criteria into investment decisions is a practical way to align portfolios with values. Companies that adhere to strict ESG practices are often seen as more sustainable and responsible, making them attractive to discerning investors.

3. Ethical screening:

Conducting ethical screening involves excluding certain industries or companies that conflict with personal values. For example, an environmental investor may choose to avoid sectors related to fossil fuels or deforestation.

4. Impact of investing:

Impact investing involves allocating capital to businesses and projects with the intention of creating positive social or environmental impacts.

This proactive approach allows investors to directly contribute to causes they care about while potentially reaping financial returns.

1. Personal Fulfillment:

Investing in alignment with personal values provides a sense of meaning and fulfillment. Knowing that one's money supports causes that matter creates a deeper connection to the investment path.

2. Reduced Cognitive Dissonance:

Traditional investment choices can conflict with personal values, leading to cognitive dissonance. Aligning investments with values reduces internal conflict and allows investors to navigate financial decisions with clarity and confidence.

3. Resilience in Volatile Markets:

Companies with strong ESG practices are often more resilient to economic and market uncertainties. Aligning investments with sustainability and ethical considerations can contribute to a more robust and resilient investment portfolio.

4. Positive social and environmental impact:

Careful investment can lead to positive change by supporting businesses that prioritize social and environmental responsibility. This approach allows investors to actively contribute to global challenges.

Practical steps for smart money management:

1. Conducting Research:

Research is key to understanding the ESG practices of companies and funds. Use resources such as ESG ratings, sustainability reports and Socially Responsible Investment (SRI) databases to make informed decisions.

2. Consultation with financial advisors:

Seek advice from financial advisors who specialize in sustainable and responsible investing. They can help align investment strategies with personal values and provide insight into potential risks and returns.

3. Diversification with respect to values:

Diversify your portfolio by focusing on industries and sectors that align with your values. This approach helps spread risk while maintaining a commitment to ethical and sustainable investment.

4. Regular portfolio review:

Market dynamics and business practices evolve, so regular portfolio reviews are essential. Stay informed about the performance of your ESG investments and adjust your portfolio as needed to stay aligned with your values.

Challenges and Considerations:

While thoughtful money management offers many benefits, investors should also be aware of potential challenges. Balancing financial goals with values requires careful consideration, and investors may face trade-offs between returns and ethical considerations. Finding a balance that aligns with individual priorities and risk tolerance is essential.

Aligning investments with values is not just a trend; it is a fundamental shift in the way individuals approach wealth creation. Mindful money management allows investors to have a positive impact on the world while achieving financial success. By adopting principles such as ESG criteria, ethical screening and impact investing, investors can navigate the complex financial landscape with purpose and contribute to a more sustainable and responsible global economy. As the financial industry continues to evolve, integrating values into investment decisions is likely to play a key role in shaping a more informed and resilient future.

4.3 Risk Management and Mindful Decision-Making

Risk management and careful decision-making are essential components when it comes to careful money management. In the complex environment of personal finance, individuals are often faced with a variety of financial decisions that can significantly affect their well-being. This is where risk management principles and careful decision-making play a vital role in ensuring a secure and sustainable financial future.

Understanding Risk Management:

Risk management involves the identification, assessment and prioritization of risks, followed by the coordinated and economical use of resources to minimize, control and monitor the impact of those risks. In personal finance, risk can take many forms, including market fluctuations, unexpected expenses, job loss or health problems. Effective management of these risks requires a proactive approach that includes a deep understanding of one's financial situation, goals and external factors that may affect them.

When it comes to careful money management, individuals need to assess their risk tolerance – the ability to withstand fluctuations in financial markets without making impulsive decisions. A balanced and diversified investment portfolio is often a key element in reducing risk. Diversification spreads investments across different assets and reduces the impact of an underperforming investment on the overall portfolio. This is a basic risk management strategy that is consistent with the principle of not putting all your eggs in one basket.

In addition, an emergency fund is a tangible expression of risk management. This financial reserve provides a safety net in case of unexpected expenses or loss of income. By being prepared for contingencies, individuals can navigate challenges without jeopardizing their overall financial stability.

Conscious decision making in money management: Mindful decision-making involves a deliberate and thoughtful approach to financial choices. It requires individuals to be aware of their financial goals, values, and the potential consequences of their decisions. One of the key aspects of careful decision-making when managing money is avoiding impulsive behavior driven by emotions. Emotional decision-making can lead to financial decisions that deviate from long-term goals.

Budgeting is a basic practice in prudent money management. Budgeting involves careful planning and allocation of funds for various expenses, savings and investments. Serves as a blueprint for financial decisions and ensures spending is aligned with priorities and goals. Regularly reviewing and adjusting the budget allows individuals to stay on track and adapt to changing circumstances.

Setting clear financial goals is another essential element of thoughtful decision-making. Whether it's saving for a home, financing education, or planning for retirement, well-defined goals provide direction and purpose for financial decisions. Mindful money management involves regularly reassessing these goals to ensure they remain relevant and achievable.

Mindful decision-making also includes making a conscious choice to invest in financial education. With a better understanding of investment options, market dynamics and financial planning strategies, individuals are empowered to make informed decisions. This knowledge equips them to navigate the complexities of the financial landscape with confidence and resilience.

Integration of risk management and careful decision-making:

Integrating risk management and careful decision-making is an effective approach to achieving financial well-being. This involves aligning risk management strategies with prudent money management principles to create a holistic and sustainable financial plan.

For example, when choosing investments, individuals can exercise careful decision-making by thoroughly researching and understanding the risks associated with each option. This includes considering factors such as historical performance, market trends and the alignment of the investment with their financial goals. At the same time, risk management comes into play by diversifying the investment portfolio to minimize the impact of the underperformance of each individual investment.

Additionally, individuals can take a mindful approach to their emergency fund. Instead of seeing it as just a financial measure, they can see it as a tool for peace of mind. This shifts the perspective from a reactive response to unforeseen events to a proactive stance that contributes to overall financial well-being.

Regularly reassessing financial goals is another area where the integration of risk management and careful decision-making is valuable. Changes in personal circumstances, economic conditions or the investment environment may require adjustments to the original financial plan. Being aware of these potential changes allows individuals to proactively manage risk and stay on track toward their goals.

In short, effective financial management involves a symbiotic relationship between risk management and careful decision-making. The dynamic nature of personal finance requires individuals to be proactive, adaptable and informed. By incorporating these principles into their financial practices, individuals can confidently navigate the complexities of the financial landscape and build a resilient foundation for their future.

4.4 Long-Term Planning with Mindful Investing

Long-term planning is a fundamental aspect of achieving financial stability and success. Combined with careful investing, it becomes an effective strategy for efficient and sustainable money management. This approach involves careful consideration of one's financial goals, risk tolerance and the impact of investment decisions on both personal well-being and the wider community. In this discussion, we will delve into the principles of long-term planning with prudent investing and explore how it contributes to a holistic and purposeful approach to money management.

Understanding long-term planning

Long-term planning is the foundation on which financial security is built. It involves setting specific, measurable, achievable, relevant and time-bound (SMART) goals. These goals can include various aspects of life, such as education, home ownership, retirement, or philanthropy. Long-term planning requires individuals to assess their current financial situation, identify future needs, and develop a plan to achieve those goals over a longer period of time. One of the key components of long-term planning is the creation of a diversified investment portfolio. Diversification helps spread risk across different asset classes and reduces the impact of poor performance in any single investment. This is where the concept of conscious investing becomes essential.

Mindful investing defined

Mindful investing goes beyond simply seeking financial returns. It involves a conscious and thoughtful approach to investment decisions that takes into account not only economic factors, but also the social and environmental impacts of those decisions. Mindful investors consider the ethical, social and governance (ESG) aspects of their investments and align their portfolios with their values and principles.

Integrating conscious investing into long-term planning

1. Values-Based Investment Choices:

Mindful investing in the context of long-term planning starts with aligning your investments with your personal values. This could include avoiding companies involved in industries that are considered harmful to society or the environment. Instead, investors can choose to support businesses with strong ethical practices and positive social contributions.

2. Sustainable and responsible investments:

Long-term planning includes recognizing the importance of sustainable and responsible investment. Companies that prioritize environmental sustainability, social responsibility and good governance are more likely to overcome economic uncertainties and contribute to a more stable and fairer future.

3. Risk management with social impact:

Mindful investors consider not only the financial risks, but also the social impact of their investment decisions. This approach involves understanding the potential consequences of supporting certain industries or companies, whether it concerns human rights, labor practices or community well-being.

4. Community and Philanthropic Investments:

Long-term planning goes beyond personal financial goals and includes a broader sense of responsibility. Mindful investors can allocate a portion of their portfolios to community development projects or philanthropic initiatives, contributing to positive change while potentially offering financial returns.

The benefits of long-term planning with sensible investing

1. Sustainable Wealth Creation:

By incorporating conscious investing into long-term planning, individuals can build wealth in a sustainable way. This includes making decisions that not only generate financial returns, but also contribute to a healthier, fairer and more environmentally conscious world.

2. Reducing financial stress:

Long-term planning coupled with careful investing helps reduce financial stress by providing a clear plan and sense of purpose. Knowing that investments align with personal values and contribute positively to society can improve overall financial well-being.

3. Positive social and environmental impact:

Mindful investors have a role to play in driving positive change. Through their investment decisions, they encourage businesses to adopt ethical practices, contribute to community development and prioritize environmental sustainability, thereby promoting a more responsible corporate environment.

4. Compliance with Evolving Values:

Long-term planning with careful investing allows individuals to adapt their financial strategies to evolving values. As societal norms and priorities change, investors can adjust their portfolios to stay in line with their principles and ensure a lasting sense of their financial journey.

Challenges and considerations

1. Market Volatility:

Careful investing can face challenges during periods of market volatility. However, the long-term perspective of planning encourages investors to weather short-term fluctuations and focus on overall positive impact and alignment with their values.

2. Availability of information:

Gathering comprehensive information about the social and environmental practices of each potential investment can be challenging. However, the growing emphasis on transparency and ESG reporting is gradually improving the availability of this information for investors.

3. Balancing Risk and Rewards:

Striking a balance between risk management and financial return remains a critical consideration. Astute investors must assess whether their portfolios effectively manage risk while offering the potential for long-term growth.

Long-term planning with careful investing is a dynamic and purpose-driven approach to money management. By incorporating values, ethics and social considerations into investment decisions, individuals can create wealth that aligns with their principles and contributes positively to society. This holistic approach not only promotes financial well-being, but also plays a key role in shaping a more sustainable and just future for individuals and communities. As the financial landscape continues to evolve, the synergy between long-term planning and mindful investing becomes increasingly important and offers a path to financial success with meaningful impact.

Chapter 5. Mindful Financial Planning for the Future

Mindful financial planning for the future is a holistic approach to managing your finances with keen awareness of the present and thoughtful consideration of your long-term goals. This practice involves cultivating a mindful attitude toward money, making intentional choices, and developing a sustainable financial strategy that aligns with your values and aspirations.

Understanding Mindful Financial Planning:
Careful financial planning begins with a deep understanding of your current financial situation. Take the time to assess your income, expenses, assets and debts. Mindfulness encourages you to be fully present during this process and avoid judgment or attachment to financial outcomes. By acknowledging your financial reality without

unnecessary stress, you can make clearer decisions about how to move forward.

Cultivating mindful money habits:
Mindful money management involves developing healthy financial habits rooted in awareness and intention. This includes creating a budget that reflects your values and priorities. Regularly tracking your expenses will help you stay on top of your spending patterns, allowing you to make adjustments in line with your financial goals.

Practicing gratitude for your financial resources, no matter how limited, is another essential aspect of mindful money habits. This shift in perspective promotes contentment and reduces the urge to pursue excessive materialism. Mindful spending, guided by a deliberate consideration of needs versus wants, allows you to allocate resources more effectively.

Building an emergency fund with awareness:
One of the cornerstones of careful financial planning is the establishment of an emergency fund. Rather than seeing it as a safety net for

unforeseen circumstances, think of it as a way to bring peace and stability to your financial life. Carefully contribute to your emergency fund and gradually build it to cover three to six months of living expenses.

Approaching emergency fund contributions with prudence means recognizing the value of financial security without succumbing to anxiety. This practice instills discipline and resilience and ensures that unexpected financial problems don't derail your overall financial well-being.

Careful investing for long-term growth:

Investing is a critical part of sound financial planning for the future. Taking a long-term perspective when it comes to investing is consistent with the principles of mindfulness. Instead of being swayed by short-term market fluctuations, focus on the long-term goals you want to achieve.

Diversification is the key to smart investing. Spread your investments across different asset classes to reduce risk and increase long-term stability. Regularly review and rebalance your portfolio, keeping in mind changes in your financial goals, risk tolerance and market conditions.

Mindful debt management:
Mindful financial planning extends to debt management. Be aware of the debt you have and try to minimize high interest debt. When dealing with existing debts, approach repayment with a calm and measured mindset. Prioritize high-interest debt while keeping minimum payments on others.

Mindfulness encourages facing financial problems with an open and non-judgmental attitude. Instead of looking at debt as a source of stress, see it as an opportunity to grow and learn. Develop a realistic and sustainable debt repayment plan that aligns with your overall financial goals.

Aligning finances with values:
Mindful financial planning involves aligning your financial decisions with your values and life purpose. Think about what's really important to you and use this overview to guide your financial decisions. Whether it's supporting causes you believe in through charitable giving or investing in

experiences over possessions, incorporating your values into your financial plan adds deeper meaning to your journey.

Mindfulness when setting financial goals:

Setting financial goals is an integral part of careful financial planning. Take the time to clearly define your short-term and long-term goals. Be specific, measurable and realistic in your goal setting process. Notice and revise your goals as your financial situation evolves.

Breaking down large goals into smaller, achievable steps promotes a sense of accomplishment and motivates further progress. Mindfulness reminds us to value the journey as much as the destination and celebrate the milestones along the way.

Mindful approach to financial challenges:

Life is unpredictable and financial problems are inevitable. Careful financial planning equips you with the resilience to face these challenges without panicking. Whether it's a job loss, unexpected medical expenses, or a market downturn, mindfulness helps you respond to these situations with a clear mind and a steady hand.

Maintain an emergency fund that will provide a buffer during challenging times. Carefully assess your options and seek support and advice if needed. By approaching financial challenges with a calm and collected mindset, you can navigate them more effectively and minimize the impact on your long-term financial well-being.

The role of mindfulness in financial decision-making:

Mindful financial planning isn't just about the numbers; it's about cultivating a healthy relationship with money. Mindfulness brings awareness to the emotional and psychological aspects of financial decision-making. It encourages you to stop, think, and make decisions that align with your values, rather than succumbing to impulsive or emotionally motivated decisions.

Practice careful decision-making by allowing yourself the space to evaluate the potential consequences of financial decisions. Consider the impact on your overall well-being, relationships, and long-term goals. Mindfulness allows you to make choices that align with your larger life goals.

Mindful reflection and continuous improvement:
Regular reflection is a crucial aspect of careful financial planning. Set aside time regularly to review your financial goals, progress, and challenges. Carefully evaluate whether your current financial strategies are still aligned with your values and aspirations.

Adopt a growth mindset and realize that financial wellness is an evolving journey. Learn from both successes and failures and adjust your approach as needed. Mindful reflection promotes a sense of self-awareness and allows you to make intentional decisions that support your continued financial growth.

Mindful financial planning for the future is a dynamic and empowering approach to managing your money. By cultivating mindfulness in your financial habits, you can navigate the complexities of personal finance with clarity, purpose, and resilience. From budgeting and investing to managing debt and setting goals, mindfulness provides the foundation for sustainable and fulfilling finances

5.1 Setting Mindful Financial Goals

Setting conscious financial goals is a crucial step to achieving financial stability and cultivating a healthy relationship with money. Mindful money management involves making conscious decisions, being aware of your spending patterns, and aligning your financial goals with your own values and priorities. In this comprehensive guide, we'll explore the importance of setting conscious financial goals, the steps involved, and the positive impact it can have on your overall well-being.

Understanding Mindful Money Management
Mindful money management goes beyond traditional budgeting and savings. It involves a deep understanding of your financial habits, emotions and attitudes towards money. By being mindful, you can develop a more intentional and purposeful approach to your finances.

1. Clarity and Focus:

Careful financial goals provide a clear picture of your financial aspirations. This clarity will help you focus on what is truly important to you and prevent impulsive decisions that may deviate from your long-term goals.

2. Align with Values:

Setting conscious financial goals involves aligning your spending and saving habits with your core values. This alignment promotes a sense of fulfillment and purpose and ensures that your financial decisions reflect your personal beliefs and priorities.

3. Reducing financial stress:

Mindful money management reduces financial stress by encouraging a proactive rather than reactive approach. When you have well-defined goals, you can effectively plan and allocate resources, minimizing the anxiety associated with financial uncertainty.

1. Self-reflection:

Start by thinking about your values, priorities and long-term aspirations. Consider how your financial decisions align with these aspects of your life. This introspective process lays the foundation for setting goals that resonate with your true self.

2. Define clear goals:

Clearly define your financial goals. Whether it's saving for housing, education or retirement, frame your goals in specific, measurable, achievable, relevant and time-bound (SMART) terms. This precision helps in creating a plan for success.

3. Prioritize Goals:

Prioritize your financial goals based on their meaning to you. Be aware of short-term and long-term goals and create a hierarchy focused on what needs immediate attention while keeping the bigger picture in mind.

4. Create an action plan:

Develop a detailed action plan for each goal. Break larger goals down into smaller, manageable tasks. This step-by-step approach makes it easy to track progress and stay motivated throughout the journey.

5. Allocate resources wisely:

Assess your current financial situation and allocate resources carefully. Be realistic about what you can afford and consider making adjustments to your spending habits if necessary. This process may involve cutting unnecessary expenses and redirecting funds to your goals.

6. Regular review and adjustments:

Review your financial goals regularly and make adjustments as needed. Life circumstances can change and so should your financial goals. Stay flexible and customize your plan to ensure ongoing alignment with your values and aspirations.

Positive impact of conscious financial goals

1. Better financial well-being:

Careful financial goals contribute to overall financial well-being. Achieving milestones and witnessing progress promotes a sense of accomplishment, increasing your confidence and peace of mind.

2. Reduced impulse spending:

Mindful money management helps curb impulsive spending. By becoming aware of the emotional triggers that lead to unnecessary spending, you can make conscious decisions that support your financial goals.

3. Increased Savings and Investments:

With clearly defined goals and a strategic plan, you are more likely to prioritize savings and investments. This disciplined approach builds financial resilience and prepares you for future opportunities or unexpected challenges.

4. Improved Decision Making:

Mindfulness cultivates better decision-making skills. When faced with financial choices, you can consider the potential impact on your goals and make informed and intentional decisions that align with your values.

Awareness of careful money management in everyday life

1. Mindful Spending:

Practice mindful spending by being aware of every financial transaction. Consider whether the purchase fits your goals and brings real value to your life. This awareness can lead to more intentional and satisfying spending habits.

2. Gratitude and Contentment:

Cultivate gratitude for your current financial situation, regardless of its complexity. Embracing contentment with what you have can reduce the urge to overspend and promote a healthier relationship with money.

3. Seeking professional advice:

Consider consulting with financial professionals who can provide professional advice tailored to your unique circumstances. Whether it's a financial planner or an advisor, their insights can complement your conscious money management efforts.

Setting conscious financial goals is a transformational journey that goes beyond monetary achievements. It's about understanding the deep connection between your values, emotions and financial decisions. By adopting a mindful approach to money management, you will not only secure your financial future, but also improve your overall well-being. Take time to reflect, set clear goals, and embrace a purpose-driven financial life that aligns with your aspirations.

5.2 Saving Mindfully for Emergencies and Goals

In today's fast-paced world, careful financial management has become an essential aspect of leading a stable, stress-free life. One of the key elements of careful money management is strategic saving. This includes setting aside funds not only for emergencies, but also for achieving future goals. In this comprehensive guide, we'll explore the importance of frugal savings, strategies for building an emergency fund, and approaches to achieving your financial goals with a focused, thoughtful mindset.

Understanding Mindful Money Management:
Mindful money management goes beyond just budgeting and tracking expenses. It involves a conscious and intentional approach to every financial decision, including saving. This approach requires individuals to be fully present and aware of their financial situation and make decisions that align with their values and long-term goals.

Importance of Emergency Funds:
An emergency fund acts as a financial safety net that provides a buffer in times of unexpected crises. Whether it's sudden medical expenses, car repairs, or an unexpected job loss, an emergency fund can prevent these situations from turning into long-term financial setbacks. The recommended amount for

an emergency fund is usually three to six months worth of living expenses.

Emergency Fund Building Strategies:

1. Set clear goals:
Clearly define your financial goals for building an emergency fund. Knowing why you're saving can provide motivation and focus.

2. Automate Savings:
Set up automatic transfers to your emergency fund to ensure consistency. Treating it like any other fixed expense helps in building the fund steadily.

3. Reduce unnecessary expenses:
Assess your spending habits and identify areas where you can cut back. Redirecting these funds into your emergency fund can help it grow faster.

4. Explore High Yield Savings Accounts:
Consider using high-yield savings accounts to earn more interest on your emergency fund. While

the returns may not be substantial, every bit helps in the long run.

Savings for future goals:

Beyond emergencies, careful money management includes saving for future goals, such as buying a home, starting a business, or funding education. Setting specific and realistic goals is the first step in this process.

Strategy for achieving financial goals:

1. Prioritize Goals:

Identify and prioritize your financial goals. This will help you allocate resources more efficiently and work towards one goal at a time.

2. Create a budget:

Create a detailed budget that allocates funds to different aspects of your life, including saving for specific goals. Review the budget regularly and adjust as needed.

3. Explore Investment Options:

Depending on the timeline of your goals, consider exploring investment options to potentially grow your savings faster than traditional savings accounts.

4. Regularly reassess:

Life circumstances and financial goals can change. Reassess your goals regularly and make adjustments as needed to stay on track.

The connection between mindfulness and money management:

Mindfulness means being fully present and aware in the present moment. When applied to money management, this means making intentional and conscious decisions about your finances. By practicing financial mindfulness, individuals can gain a deeper understanding of their spending habits, make more informed decisions, and cultivate a healthier relationship with money.

Saving for emergencies and goals is a cornerstone of effective money management. It takes intention, discipline and determination to align financial decisions with personal values and aspirations. By building a robust emergency fund and strategically saving for future goals, individuals can navigate financial challenges with confidence and work towards a more secure and fulfilling financial future.

5.3 Retirement Planning with a Mindful Approach

Mindful retirement planning is a holistic and intentional way to prepare for life after your active working years. In a world dominated by financial goals and wealth accumulation, incorporating mindfulness into retirement planning can bring a sense of balance, purpose, and peace. This approach encourages individuals to align their financial strategies with their values, goals and overall well-being.

Understanding Conscious Retirement Planning:

Mindful retirement planning involves a deep awareness of one's financial situation, values and life preferences. Instead of simply focusing on accumulating a specific amount of money, individuals who care about careful money management take the time to think about what retirement really means to them. This may include consideration of factors such as desired activities, travel plans, family responsibilities and community involvement.

By taking a thoughtful approach, individuals can create a retirement plan that goes beyond just numbers. It becomes a personalized road map that reflects their unique aspirations and ensures that the financial aspect of retirement is aligned with a fulfilling and purpose-driven life.

Mindful Money Management Principles

1. Awareness and reflection:

   - Take time to reflect on your personal values, priorities and life goals.

   - Understand the emotional aspects of money and how they affect financial decisions.

- Cultivate awareness of spending, distinguishing between needs and wants.

2. Determining intentional goals:

- Define specific and realistic retirement goals based on personal aspirations.
- Prioritize goals that bring fulfillment, whether they involve travel, hobbies or community involvement.
- Consider the impact of financial decisions on overall well-being and happiness.

3. Budgeting and Spending:

- Create a detailed budget that takes into account both short-term and long-term financial needs.
- Practice mindful spending by making conscious decisions in line with personal values.
- Regularly review and adjust the budget to ensure alignment with evolving priorities.

4. Risk Management with Peace of Mind:

- Approach investment decisions with a balanced and calm mindset.

- Diversify investments to manage risk and adapt to market fluctuations.

- Regularly evaluate risk tolerance and adjust investment strategies accordingly.

5. Focus on health and well-being:

- Prioritize physical and mental health, as they directly affect the quality of life in retirement.

- Include health care costs in financial planning and explore wellness practices for a balanced lifestyle.

- Consider possible lifestyle changes that contribute to overall well-being during retirement.

The Role of Mindfulness in Financial Decision Making

Mindfulness practices such as meditation and mindful breathing can play a key role in navigating the complexities of retirement planning. By incorporating mindfulness into their daily lives, individuals can cultivate a sense of clarity and focus, reducing the stress and anxiety associated with financial decision-making.

1. Emotional Resilience:

- Mindfulness helps individuals develop emotional resilience and makes it easier for them to manage financial problems.

- Emotional intelligence promotes a healthier relationship with money, reducing impulsive decisions driven by fear or greed.

2. Present Moment Awareness:

- Mindfulness promotes living in the present moment and prevents excessive worry about the future.

- Being present with financial decisions allows for a more deliberate and thoughtful approach to retirement planning.

3. Stress Reduction:

- Financial worries can be a significant source of stress. Mindfulness practices offer powerful tools for managing and reducing stress.

- Reducing stress contributes to better decision-making and overall well-being during the retirement years.

4. Improved Decision Making:

- Mindful individuals are more likely to make decisions in line with their values, leading to greater satisfaction in retirement.

- Enhanced self-awareness supports the ability to make informed and deliberate financial decisions.

Mindful Retirement Planning in Practice

1. Value Based Investing:

- Align investments with personal values, supporting companies and initiatives that resonate with individuals' beliefs.

- Consider environmental, social and governance (ESG) factors in investment decisions.

2. Lifestyle Alignment:

- Assess your desired retirement lifestyle and adjust financial plans accordingly.

- Carefully select housing options, travel plans and leisure activities that align with personal preferences and values.

3. Flexible financial strategy:

- Adopt flexibility in financial strategies to accommodate unexpected changes in health, family or market conditions.

- Reassess financial goals regularly and make adjustments as needed.

4. Mindful Spending in Retirement:

- Prioritize spending on experiences and activities that bring joy and fulfillment.

- Exercise sparingly and avoid overconsumption that can lead to financial stress.

Challenges and Considerations:

While taking a mindful approach to retirement planning offers numerous benefits, it is essential to be aware of the potential challenges and considerations.

1. External pressures:

- Financial decisions can be influenced by societal expectations and external pressures.

Mindfulness helps individuals stay true to their values despite external influences.

2. Market Volatility:

- Economic uncertainties and market volatility can cause concern. Mindful investors approach market fluctuations with a long-term perspective and disciplined decision-making.

3. Long-term care planning:

- Addressing potential long-term care needs requires careful consideration. Mindful planning includes exploring health care options and securing financial resources.

4. Legacy Planning:

- Mindful retirement planning extends to older considerations. Individuals may choose to incorporate charitable giving or support for future generations into their financial plan.

Mindful retirement planning is a journey that involves self-discovery, intentional goal-setting, and a commitment to living a fulfilling life in your retirement years. By incorporating mindfulness into financial decision-making, individuals can create a retirement plan that not only sustains them financially, but also enriches their lives on a deeper level. It's a holistic approach that considers mind, body and spirit, ensuring that retirement is a chapter full of purpose, joy and peace of mind.

5.4 Mindful Strategies for Debt Management

In an era of financial stress, adopting thoughtful debt management strategies has become essential to maintaining a healthy financial life. Mindful money management goes beyond traditional budgeting; it involves a holistic approach that considers the emotional and psychological aspects of the relationship with money. In this context, incorporating mindfulness into debt management practices can lead to more sustainable and effective outcomes.

Understanding Mindful Money Management

Mindful money management involves cultivating awareness and consciousness in financial decision-making. It's about being fully present in the moment and making informed decisions rather than reacting impulsively to financial challenges. When applied to debt management, this approach can help individuals develop a healthier relationship with their finances, paving the way to long-term financial well-being.

Recognizing the emotional aspect of debt

Debt is not just a financial burden; it also has emotional weight. Acknowledging and understanding these emotions is a fundamental aspect of mindful debt management. Many individuals experience stress, anxiety or guilt associated with their debt, which can significantly affect their overall well-being. Mindfulness encourages individuals to face these emotions and promotes a sense of control and empowerment over their financial situation.

Creating a conscious budget:

One of the basic steps in careful money management is creating a careful budget. Unlike traditional budgets that only focus on numbers, mindful budgeting involves an awareness of spending and values. This includes regularly reviewing and reassessing financial goals, aligning spending with personal values, and making intentional decisions to prioritize needs over wants.

Practicing gratitude and contentment:
In a consumerist society, the constant pursuit of more can lead to overspending and debt accumulation. Mindful debt management involves cultivating gratitude and contentment with what one has. This does not mean settling for little, but rather appreciating and finding joy in the present moment. This shift in thinking can naturally reduce unnecessary spending and help reduce debt accumulation.

Careful decision-making in financial transactions:
Every financial decision, big or small, plays a role in overall debt management. Mindfulness encourages individuals to approach financial transactions with a

clear understanding of their consequences. This includes asking crucial questions before making a purchase, such as whether it is in line with long-term goals and whether it is a necessity or a momentary desire. By incorporating mindfulness into decision-making, individuals can make choices that support their financial well-being.

Building an emergency fund with awareness:
A fundamental aspect of thoughtful debt management is building and maintaining an emergency fund. This financial safety net provides protection against unexpected expenses and reduces dependence on credit in times of crisis. Mindfulness comes into play when individuals approach building an emergency fund with a sense of purpose and commitment. Regular contributions, even if small, contribute to financial stability and a sense of control over unforeseen circumstances.

Mindful communication about finances:
Effective communication is the key to managing household finances. Mindful money management extends to open and honest discussions about

financial goals, challenges and strategies. Couples or families who practice sensitive communication can work together to address debt-related issues and create a supportive environment that encourages responsible financial behavior.

Mindfulness in debt repayment strategies:
When it comes to paying off debt, a thoughtful approach involves creating a realistic and sustainable repayment plan. Mindfulness encourages the individual to break down large goals into smaller, manageable steps and celebrate accomplishments. This approach not only provides a sense of progress, but also minimizes the burden that is often associated with significant debt.

Look carefully for professional guidance:
In some cases, seeking professional help is a conscious step towards debt management. Whether through financial advisors, debt counselors, or educational resources, mindfulness plays a role in choosing and engaging with these services. Being fully present in these interactions allows individuals to absorb and effectively use

advice and make informed decisions about their financial future.

Cultivating financial mindfulness as a lifelong practice:
Mindful money management is not a one-time solution, but a lifelong practice. Cultivating financial mindfulness involves constant self-reflection, adaptability, and a willingness to learn from both successes and failures. Integrating mindfulness into everyday financial habits ultimately leads to a more sustainable and resilient approach to debt management.

In pursuit of financial wellness, it is essential to incorporate conscious strategies into your debt management practices. Mindful money management goes beyond numbers and addresses the emotional and psychological aspects of your relationship with money. By embracing mindfulness, individuals can gain a deeper understanding of their financial behavior, make intentional decisions, and work towards a more stable and fulfilling financial future.

Conclusion

Mindful money management is a holistic approach to financial well-being that goes beyond traditional budgeting and investment strategies. By incorporating the principles of mindfulness into our financial practices, we cultivate a deeper awareness of our financial behavior, values, and the impact of our decisions on our present and future selves. This contextual conclusion explores key aspects of money management and highlights its benefits, challenges and potential for positive change in individual and societal financial environments.

At its core, careful money management encourages individuals to develop a conscious and intentional relationship with money. This includes being fully present in financial activities such as budgeting, spending, saving and investing. By practicing mindfulness, individuals gain insight into their financial habits, identifying patterns that may be counterproductive or driven by unconscious impulses. This increased awareness allows individuals to make informed decisions that align with their values and long-term goals.

One of the basic principles of conscious money management is the cultivation of gratitude for financial resources. This means appreciating what one has rather than constantly striving for more. By acknowledging and expressing gratitude for financial blessings, individuals can promote positive thinking and reduce the tendency to impulsive or excessive spending. This shift in perspective promotes contentment and can contribute to a healthier relationship with money.

In addition, mindful money management emphasizes the importance of setting clear financial goals that align with our values and aspirations. Mindful individuals take the time to think about their priorities, whether it's saving for education, buying a home, or achieving financial independence. Setting realistic and meaningful goals provides a sense of purpose and motivates individuals to make intentional financial decisions that support their goals.

However, the path to careful money management is not without problems. In a rapidly changing and consumer-oriented society, external pressures can influence individuals to prioritize immediate gratification over long-term financial well-being. The pervasive influence of marketing, societal expectations, and the constant bombardment of consumer culture can make it challenging for individuals to stay true to their conscious financial principles.

Overcoming these challenges requires sustained commitment and a willingness to constantly reassess your financial habits. Mindful money management involves regularly examining financial options and adjusting them to fit evolving life circumstances and priorities. This adaptability is critical to navigating the dynamic nature of personal finance and ensures that individuals remain mindful and intentional in their financial decision-making.

The intersection of mindfulness and money management goes beyond personal benefits and has the potential to promote positive social change. As individuals become more aware of their financial choices, there is a ripple effect that can affect broader economic and social systems. Mindful consumers are more likely to support businesses and practices that are in line with ethical and sustainable values and contribute to a more socially responsible and environmentally conscious economy.

In addition, the practice of mindful money management can address systemic issues related to financial literacy and inequality. By promoting financial education and mindfulness practices, individuals from diverse socioeconomic backgrounds can gain the tools and knowledge needed to make informed financial decisions. This empowerment has the potential to reduce the wealth gap and create more equitable opportunities for economic development.

Mindful money management is a transformative approach that goes beyond traditional financial strategies. By incorporating the principles of mindfulness into our relationship with money, we can gain a deeper understanding of our financial behavior, cultivate gratitude, set meaningful goals, and manage the challenges of a consumer society. This intentional and holistic approach not only benefits individuals on a personal level, but also has the potential to contribute to positive societal change by promoting a more ethical, sustainable and fair financial environment. As we continue to navigate the complexities of the modern financial world, embracing mindful money management can be the key to achieving lasting financial well-being and creating a more prosperous and harmonious society.

The art of careful money management goes beyond mere financial success; it is a holistic approach that connects wealth with well-being. Finding a balance between these two aspects is not only achievable, but also necessary for a fulfilling and meaningful life.

As we navigate the complex landscape of personal finance, it is clear that true prosperity goes beyond the accumulation of monetary assets. Mindful money management challenges us to consider the impact of our financial decisions on our overall well-being, emphasizing the interconnectedness of wealth and happiness.

Along the way, we explored the importance of setting clear financial goals in line with our values and aspirations. By understanding the purpose behind our financial activities, we are empowered to make intentional decisions that lead to both financial success and personal fulfillment.

In addition, cultivating mindfulness in our financial practices includes being present in our financial transactions and decisions. Whether budgeting, investing, or making purchasing decisions, a mindful approach encourages us to be aware of the consequences of our actions and the values they reflect.

The concept of mindful spending is proving to be a powerful tool that redirects our attention from impulse purchases to intentional and meaningful spending. This shift not only contributes to sound financial management, but also increases our sense of satisfaction and contentment and promotes a positive relationship between wealth and well-being.

Additionally, the importance of building a strong financial base cannot be overstated. Mindful money management encourages us to prioritize savings, emergency funds, and investments that align with our long-term goals. This strategic approach not only secures our financial future, but provides a sense of security that positively affects our overall well-being.

When we consider the interconnectedness of wealth and well-being, the role of gratitude as a transformative force emerges. Practicing gratitude for the resources and opportunities we have cultivates a positive mindset that transcends the financial situation. It allows us to appreciate the abundance in our lives and promotes contentment regardless of the size of our bank accounts.

In the search for a balanced financial and personal life, the importance of conscious consumption becomes apparent. Mindful money management encourages us to assess our needs and wants and encourages conscious decisions that align with our values. This shift not only contributes to financial prudence, but also minimizes the environmental and social impact of our consumption patterns and reinforces the ethical dimension of wealth.

The connection between financial health and mental well-being is undeniable. Mindful money management emphasizes the importance of maintaining a healthy relationship with money to reduce stress and promote mental well-being. By addressing financial challenges with a calm and collected mindset, we empower ourselves to overcome obstacles and build resilience in the face of economic uncertainties.

Mindful money management is a transformative approach that transcends traditional notions of financial success. It challenges us to rethink our relationship with money and encourages intentional choices that harmonize wealth with well-being. By setting clear goals, practicing mindful spending, building a solid financial foundation, and embracing gratitude and mindful consumption, we embark on a journey that not only improves our financial situation, but enriches our lives in profound ways. Achieving a balance between wealth and well-being is not just a desire, but a tangible and rewarding reality within our reach.